AF599117

COOL CARS
MASERATI
GRANCABRIO
EPIC
BY KAITLYN DULING
BELLWETHER MEDIA ››› MINNEAPOLIS, MN

EPIC BOOKS are no ordinary books. They burst with intense action, high-speed heroics, and shadows of the unknown. Are you ready for an Epic adventure?

This edition first published in 2025 by Bellwether Media, Inc.

Library of Congress Cataloging-in-Publication Data

LC record for Maserati GranCabrio available at: https://lccn.loc.gov/2024039221

Editor: Rachael Barnes Designer: Gabriel Hilger

Printed in the United States of America, North Mankato, MN.

TABLE OF CONTENTS

DROP-TOP DRIVING	4
ALL ABOUT THE GRANCABRIO	6
PARTS OF THE GRANCABRIO	12
THE GRANCABRIO'S FUTURE	20
GLOSSARY	22
TO LEARN MORE	23
INDEX	24

DROP-TOP DRIVING

A gentle wind blows. The Maserati GranCabrio cuts through the air. It drives smoothly down a country road.

The driver uses a control on the **touch screen**. The GranCabrio's roof folds down. Time for an open-air drive!

ALL ABOUT THE GRANCABRIO

BUILT BY HAND

Maserati cars have always been made by hand in Italy. Fans travel from around the world to tour the factory!

EARLY MASERATI CAR

Three Maserati brothers decided to form their own car company. Alfieri, Ettore, and Ernesto started Maserati in Italy in 1914.

Today, Maserati makes **luxury** cars and race cars. The MC12 and Ghibli are famous **models**.

in shape and power.

Both are grand touring cars. They are built to drive fast over long distances.

GRANCABRIO BASICS

YEAR FIRST MADE	2010
COST	starts around $200,000
HOW MANY MADE	currently in production

FEATURES

grille

soft top

touch screen

The GranCabrio was first sold from 2010 to 2019. It returned in 2024.

NAME GAME

Cabrio is a nickname for convertibles. Other nicknames are drop-top, roadster, spyder, and cabriolet.

This four-seat convertible was originally released in one **trim** called the Trofeo. The name means "trophy" in Italian.

PARTS OF THE GRANCABRIO

The GranCabrio has a Nettuno **V6 engine**. Maserati builds each of these engines by hand.

Air moves through the **grille** to cool the engine. A large **badge** on the grille marks the car as a Maserati.

ENGINE SPECS

TWIN-TURBO NETTUNO V6 ENGINE

TOP SPEED 196 miles (315 kilometers) per hour

0-60 TIME 3.4 seconds

HORSEPOWER 542 hp

BADGE
GRILLE

Drivers control the soft top from a touch screen. The top opens in 14 seconds!

SOFT TOP

SIZE CHART

By turning a dial, the car can switch between four **drive modes**. They change the GranCabrio's sound and feel.

It can get cold and windy when a convertible's top is down. The GranCabrio has neck warmers on the seats.

A **wind stopper** can be added behind the front seats. It slows down the wind speed inside the car.

The GranCabrio Folgore hit the road in 2025. The word *folgore* means "lightning" in Italian.

The Folgore is powered by a **battery** and runs on three **electric motors**.

TOP OPTIONS

The GranCabrio's top comes in five different colors. Drivers can choose their favorite from black, blue, red, tan, and gray.

THE GRANCABRIO'S FUTURE »

Fans hope Maserati will release more GranCabrio trims. For now, the company plans to build more electric cars.

Some Maseratis will race in **Formula E**. More winning cars may be on the way!

MASERATI FACTORY

MASERATI FORMULA E CAR

GLOSSARY

badge—a sign to show that a person or thing belongs to a certain group

battery—a part that supplies electric energy to a car

convertible—related to a car with a folding or soft roof

drive modes—settings in cars that change how the car drives for different tasks

electric motors—machines that give something the power to move by using electricity

Formula E—a type of electric car racing

grille—a set of bars that covers an opening on the front of a car; the grille allows air to enter and exit the engine.

luxury—having a high level of comfort

models—specific kinds of cars

touch screen—a display on which people can select options by touching the screen

trim—a model of a car with a specific set of features and equipment

V6 engine—an engine with 6 cylinders arranged in the shape of a "V"

wind stopper—a panel attached to the back of a convertible's front seats; wind stoppers reduce wind and noise in a car.

TO LEARN MORE

AT THE LIBRARY

Colby, Jennifer. *Maserati.* Ann Arbor, Mich.: Cherry Lake Publishing, 2023.

Duling, Kaitlyn. *Maserati MC20.* Minneapolis, Minn.: Bellwether Media, 2024.

Hamilton, S.L. *Maserati.* Minneapolis, Minn.: Abdo Publishing, 2023.

ON THE WEB

FACTSURFER

Factsurfer.com gives you a safe, fun way to find more information.

1. Go to www.factsurfer.com.
2. Enter “Maserati GranCabrio” into the search box and click 🔍.
3. Select your book cover to see a list of related content.

INDEX

badge, 12, 13
basics, 9
battery, 19
colors, 19
convertible, 8, 11, 16
drive modes, 15
electric cars, 20
electric motors, 19
engine, 12
engine specs, 12
factory, 6, 20
Formula E, 20, 21
GranTurismo, 8
grille, 12, 13
history, 6, 7, 10, 18
Italy, 6, 7
Maserati (company), 6, 7, 12, 20
Maserati, Alfieri, 6
Maserati, Ernesto, 6
Maserati, Ettore, 6
models, 7, 8
name, 11, 18
neck warmers, 16
roof, 5, 14, 16, 19
seats, 16, 17
size, 14-15
touch screen, 5, 14, 15
trims, 11, 18, 19, 20
wind stopper, 17

The images in this book are reproduced through the courtesy of: Maserati, front cover, pp. 3, 4, 5, 8 (main, GranTurismo Trofeo), 9 (isolated, fabric top, grille, touch screen), 11, 12, 13, 14 (soft top, width), 15 (touch screen, dial), 16, 17, 18, 19; GP Library Limited/ Alamy, p. 6; Damian Morys, p. 7; VDWI Automotive/ Alamy, p. 10; Jack Skeens, p. 15 (length); MikeDotta, p. 20; LFP/ Alamy, p. 21.